Contents

Weblink: www.curriculumvisions.com

Many kinds of plants

Plants come in lots of shapes and sizes.

The world has lots of plants.

They are not all the same.

Some grow on land.

Some grow in water.

Some grow on other plants.

Some have prickles.

Some even eat insects!

mushroom

Moss has lots of tiny leaves.
A mushroom looks like a hat.

This ivy is a
climbing plant.

A dandelion
grows in fields.
It has yellow flowers.

Curriculum Visions **1B** Science@School

Growing plants

Curriculum Visions

Science@School

Teacher's Guide
There is a Teacher's Guide available
to accompany this book.

Dedicated Web Site
There is a wealth of supporting
material including videos and activities
available at the Professional Zone,
part of our dedicated web site:

www.CurriculumVisions.com

The Professional Zone
is a subscription zone.

A CVP Book.
First published in 2008

Copyright © 2008 Earthscape

Authors
Peter Riley, BSc, C Biol, MI Biol, PGCE,
and Brian Knapp, BSc, PhD

Senior Designer
Adele Humphries, BA, PGCE

Educational Consultant
Jan Smith (former Deputy Head of Wellfield School,
Burnley, Lancashire)

Editor
Gillian Gatehouse

Designed and produced by
EARTHSCAPE

Printed in China by
WKT Co., Ltd

Curriculum Visions Science@School
Volume 1B Growing plants
A CIP record for this book is available
from the British Library.
ISBN: 978 1 86214 254 1

Picture credits
All pictures are from the Earthscape and
ShutterStock collections.

This product is manufactured from sustainable
managed forests. For every tree cut down at least one
more is planted.

A sunflower is a tall plant
that grows in gardens.

A tree is the biggest kind of plant. It has thick branches.

Venus fly trap

This plant eats flies.
It is called a Venus fly trap.

A cactus has sharp prickles.

What plants can you see from your window?

Weblink: www.curriculumvisions.com

Where plants grow

Plants grow in lots of different places.

Some plants can grow under ice and snow on a mountain.

Grass grows on a lawn.

Weblink: www.curriculumvisions.com

Ferns grow in a wood.

ferns

A water lily grows in ponds.

Plants can grow
in your home.
This one is called
a rubber plant.

Seaweed grows in the sea.

What plants do people grow in their homes?

Weblink: www.curriculumvisions.com

The parts of a plant

Plants have roots, stems, leaves and flowers.

When you see a plant, you may just notice the flowers and the leaves.

Plants also have roots and stems.

You can see them here.

This is a geranium.

flower

stem

leaves

The roots of a houseplant are in a pot.

roots

Weblink: www.curriculumvisions.com

Some plants have bulbs. Bulbs are where the leaves grow from.

This is a daffodil.

This is a hyacinth.

You can watch leaves and roots come out of an onion if you put it in a glass of water.

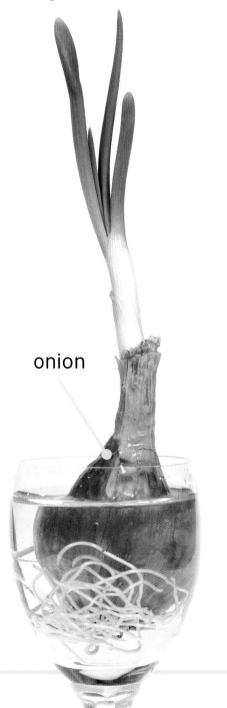

onion

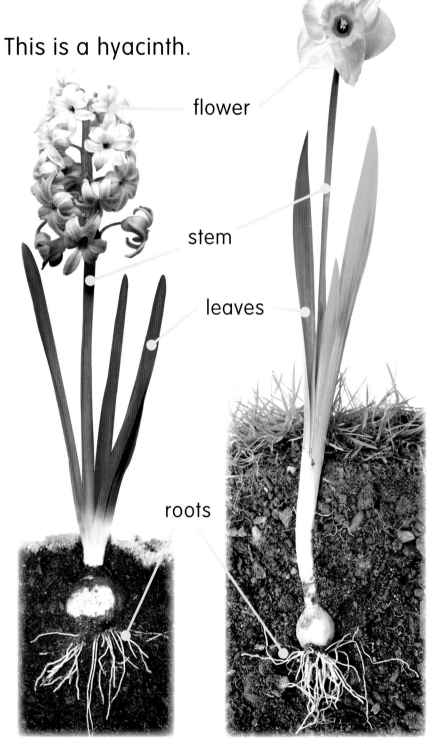

flower

stem

leaves

roots

How is a root different from a stem?

Weblink: www.curriculumvisions.com

Petals

Many flowers have petals.

Petals are thin and have bright colours. Petals make up most of a flower.

A poppy has red petals.

A buttercup has yellow petals.

poppy

buttercup

10

This rose has red petals.

sunflower

rose

This sunflower has yellow petals and green leaves.

How is a petal different from a leaf?

The roots

Roots hold plants in the ground.

Roots are under the ground. The roots stop the plant falling over. They also suck in water for the plant to grow.

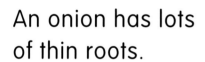

An onion has lots of thin roots.

A carrot has one long thick root.

These seedlings have many tiny roots.

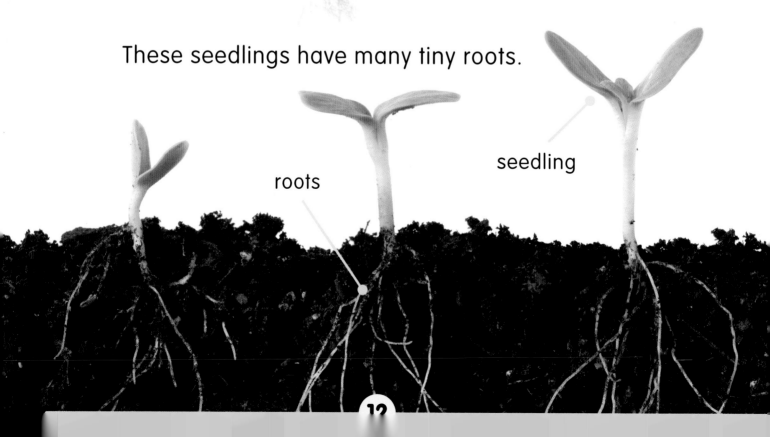

seedling

roots

A tree has lots of thick roots.

What could make a tree fall over?

Weblink: www.curriculumvisions.com

A plant grows up

Plants grow from seeds.

A seed is small and hard. Here you can see what happens as a bean seed grows into a plant.

1 A bean is a seed. When it is put in soil it soaks up water and swells.

2

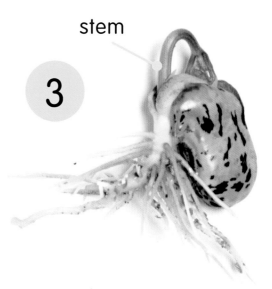

root

The root grows out of the bean seed.

stem

3

Next, the stem grows out of the bean seed.

Weblink: www.curriculumvisions.com

leaves

4 The stem grows tall
and leaves appear.

flowers

5 The bean plant grows tall
and flowers come out.

Which part of the plant grows first?

Weblink: www.curriculumvisions.com

Water, warmth and light

Plants need water, warmth and light to live.

Plants flop over when they need water.

Plants stop growing in winter when it is cold.

Plants do not grow where there is no light.

We stand flowers in water if we want them to last.

A rose taken out of water soon flops over. This is called wilting.

Plants grow well in summer when it is warm and the Sun can shine a long time each day.

Many plants do not grow in winter. It is cold and the Sun does not shine very long each day.

When do plants grow best?

17

Plants are food

We grow some plants for food.

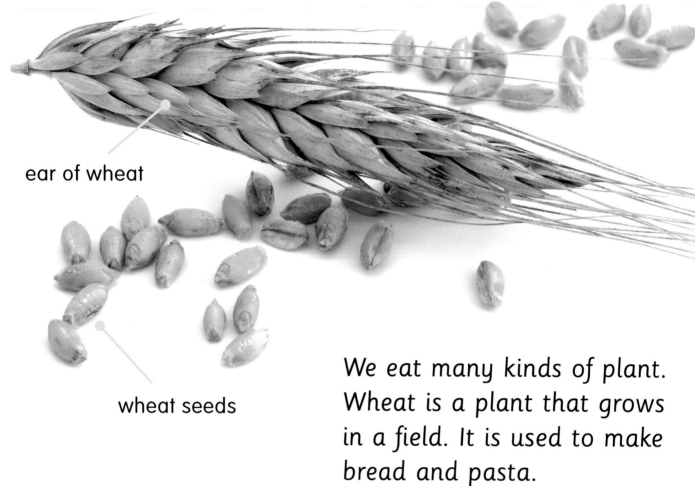

ear of wheat

wheat seeds

We eat many kinds of plant. Wheat is a plant that grows in a field. It is used to make bread and pasta.

Bread is made from wheat.

Weblink: www.curriculumvisions.com

Here are lots more plants we eat. Most of them are vegetables. Some are fruits. They all grow in fields.

Apples are a fruit. They grow on apple trees.

A collection of vegetables.

parsley

mushroom

potato

celery

Can you name some other plants that we eat?

Weblink: www.curriculumvisions.com

Common food plants

Here are some plants that we eat.

We can only eat some parts of plants. Those are the parts we see in shops.

The rest of the plant is left in the field.

Here is what some food plants look like when they are growing.

ear of wheat

Wheat is a type of grass.
We eat the seeds that
are inside the ears.
We do not eat the stalk,
the leaves or the root.

20

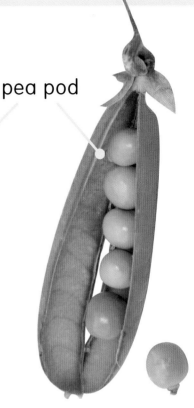

pea pod

Peas are climbing plants.
We only eat the peas inside the pods.

pumpkin pie

Pumpkins are very large vegetables.
They grow resting on the ground.
We eat the soft inside of the pumpkin.

Which part of a carrot do we eat?

Weblink: www.curriculumvisions.com

Branch

Parts of a tree which stick out from a tree trunk.

Bulb

A round part of a plant. It is made of leaves.

onion bulb cut in half

Flower

A part of the plant that makes seeds.

Fruit

The part of a plant where the seeds grow.

apricot stone

Lawn

Ground covered in grass, which is kept short with a mower.

Mushroom

A plant that is not green and does not have flowers.

Seed

Something which grows into a plant.

Seedling

A very young plant.

Wilt

Bend over or droop.

Weblink: www.curriculumvisions.com

Index